Try Something New

100 Fun & Creative Ways to Spend Time Together

Published by Neuron Publishing
www.neuronpublishing.com
www.LoveBookOnline.com

Completed: _____

#1 – Go hunting for hidden treasures

Make a list of items that you think you'd find at a garage sale or antique shop. Head out to sales in your neighborhood and see how many things you can cross off your list.

Did you work together or split up the list? _____
_____

How well did you do? What was the hardest thing to find? _____
_____

What was your favorite part? _____
_____

How would you rank this? ☆☆☆☆☆ Why? _____

1

Completed:

_____

#2 - Get the best seats in the place

Create a private backyard concert just for the two of you. Grab a blanket, some drinks, and rock out to your favorite tunes. You get to control the music, setting, and the company.

What music did you play?_____

_____

Did you share control of the music selection?_____

_____

What was your favorite part?_____

_____

How would you rank this? ☆☆☆☆☆ Why? _____

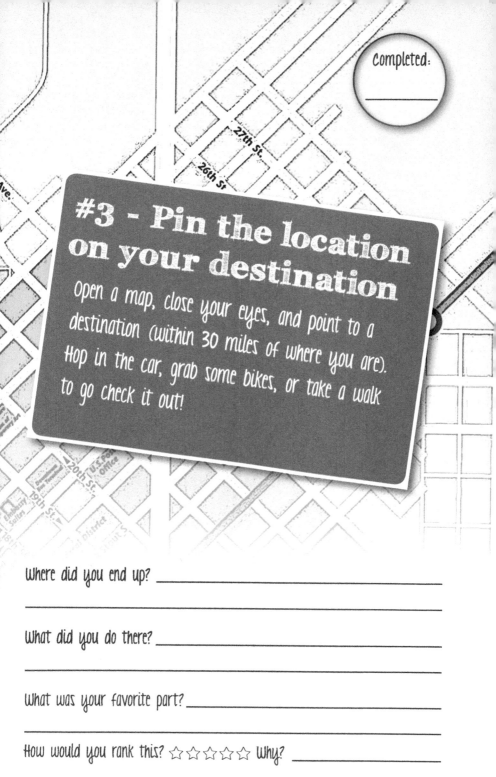

#3 - Pin the location on your destination

Open a map, close your eyes, and point to a destination (within 30 miles of where you are). Hop in the car, grab some bikes, or take a walk to go check it out!

Where did you end up? _____

_____

What did you do there? _____

_____

What was your favorite part? _____

_____

How would you rank this? ☆☆☆☆☆ Why? _____

Completed:

_____

#4 – Cozy up under the starry night sky

On the next clear night, go outside with a sky map and a comfy blanket. Lay down and try to pick out the constellations together. You won't find a more romantic setting.

What constellations were you able to see? _____

_____

Was this a good place to see the stars? _____

_____

What was your favorite part?_____

_____

How would you rank this? ☆☆☆☆☆ Why? _____

#5 - Take a trip back to a simpler time

Spend an entire evening without any modern conveniences. TV, cell phones, and computers are off limits. Turn off the lights, light some candles, and just enjoy each other's company.

What was the first thing you noticed? _____

_____

What did you learn about each other? _____

_____

What was your favorite part? _____

_____

How would you rank this? ☆☆☆☆☆ Why? _____

#6 - Test your artistic drink mixing skills

Grab whatever ingredients you think will make the custom drink that best fits your partner. Mix away and then exchange drinks and see how well you did.

Why did you choose those ingredients? _____

_____

Did you like each other's drinks? Why? _____

_____

What was your favorite part? _____

_____

How would you rank this? ☆ ☆ ☆ ☆ ☆ Why? _____

#7 - Explore with turn-by-turn navigation

Go out for a drive and see how far you can get making only right hand turns. You never know what hidden gem lies right around the next corner.

How far did you get? _____

_____

What did you see along the way? _____

_____

What was your favorite part? _____

_____

How would you rank this? ☆☆☆☆☆ Why? _____

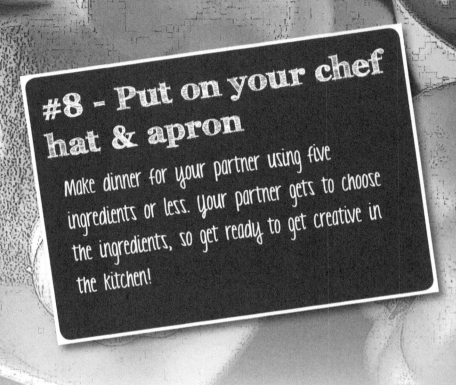

#8 – Put on your chef hat & apron

Make dinner for your partner using five ingredients or less. Your partner gets to choose the ingredients, so get ready to get creative in the kitchen!

What did you cook and how did you make it? _____

_____

How would you review what you made? _____

_____

What was your favorite part? _____

_____

How would you rank this? ☆☆☆☆☆ Why? _____

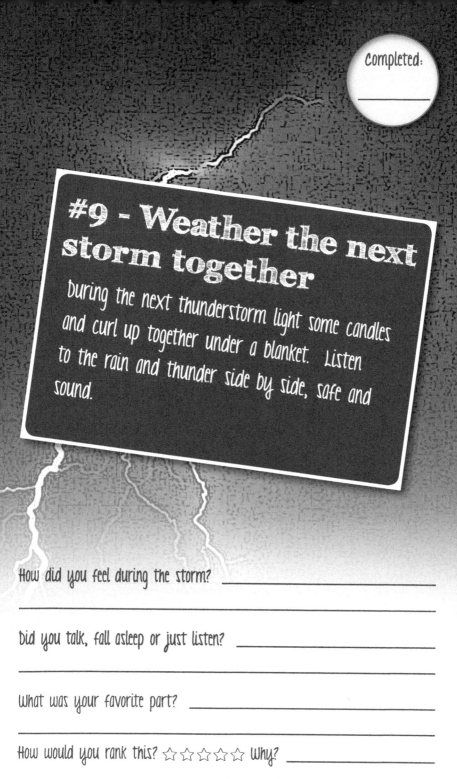

#9 - Weather the next storm together

During the next thunderstorm light some candles and curl up together under a blanket. Listen to the rain and thunder side by side, safe and sound.

How did you feel during the storm? _____

_____

Did you talk, fall asleep or just listen? _____

_____

What was your favorite part? _____

_____

How would you rank this? ☆☆☆☆☆ Why? _____

S.A.

#10 - See your area through a new lens

Grab a camera and head out for a walking tour of your neighborhood. See if you can take a picture of places or things that start with every letter of the alphabet.

Did you notice anything new? _____

_____

Which areas would you want to go back to? _____

_____

What was your favorite part? _____

_____

How would you rank this? ☆☆☆☆☆ Why? _____

#11 - Hang out like you are kids again

Clear some space in your living room and build a fort out of blankets. Put on your favorite childhood movie, pop some popcorn, and let your adult cares fade away

Were you able to let go and just have fun? _____

_____

What movie did you pick? Why? _____

_____

What was your favorite part? _____

_____

How would you rank this? ☆☆☆☆☆ Why? _____

Completed:

_____

#12 - Head west young men & women

Drive straight West (or East, if West isn't a viable option) for 45 minutes. Get out and explore wherever you end up. Bring back a souvenir of your little road trip.

Where did you end up? _____

_____

What did you do when you got there? _____

_____

What was your favorite part? _____

_____

How would you rank this? ☆ ☆ ☆ ☆ ☆ Why? _____

Completed:

_____

#13 - Name that tune in 15 seconds or less

Choose 10 of your favorite songs. Play 15 seconds of a song and see if the other person can guess the title and the artist. Switch and see who guesses the most correctly.

Who was better at naming the tunes? _____

_____

What was the hardest song to guess? _____

_____

What was your favorite part? _____

_____

How would you rank this? ☆☆☆☆☆ Why? _____

13

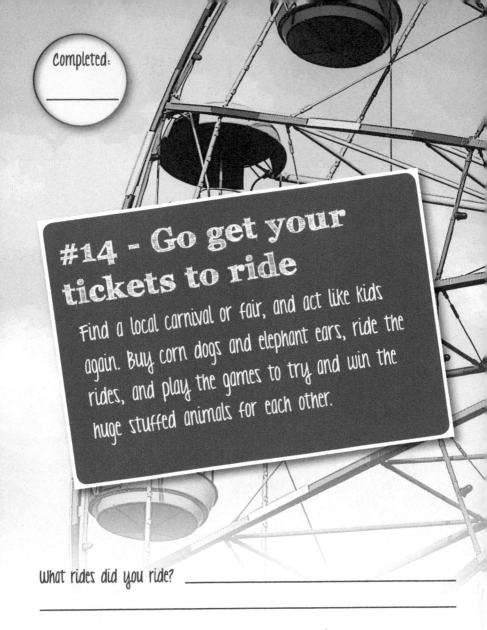

#14 - Go get your tickets to ride

Find a local carnival or fair, and act like kids again. Buy corn dogs and elephant ears, ride the rides, and play the games to try and win the huge stuffed animals for each other.

What rides did you ride? _____

_____

Did you win any of the games? What were your prizes? _____

_____

What was your favorite part? _____

_____

How would you rank this? ☆☆☆☆☆ Why? _____

14

Completed:
_____

#15 - Go on a modern day scavenger hunt

Geocaching is a great way to get outside, explore new areas, and test your navigation skills. All you need is a device with GPS. Check out www.geocaching.com for locations.

What was the most challenging part? _____
_____

How well did you work together? _____
_____

What was your favorite part? _____
_____

How would you rank this? ☆☆☆☆☆ Why? _____

#16 - Discover your own great outdoors

Camp out for the night in your own backyard. Set up a tent or put down some sleeping bags and sleep under the stars. Experience nature without leaving home.

Did you put up a tent or did you truly rough it? _____

_____

How well did you sleep? _____

_____

What was your favorite part? _____

_____

How would you rank this? ☆☆☆☆☆ Why? _____

#17 – Get in touch with your inner artist

Take an art class together. Make a mosaic, paint some pottery, or sketch a still life. Some classes even offer wine to help you get those creative juices flowing.

What kind of class did you take? _____
_____

What did you make? Did you make it together? _____
_____

What was your favorite part? _____
_____

How would you rank this? ☆☆☆☆☆ Why? _____

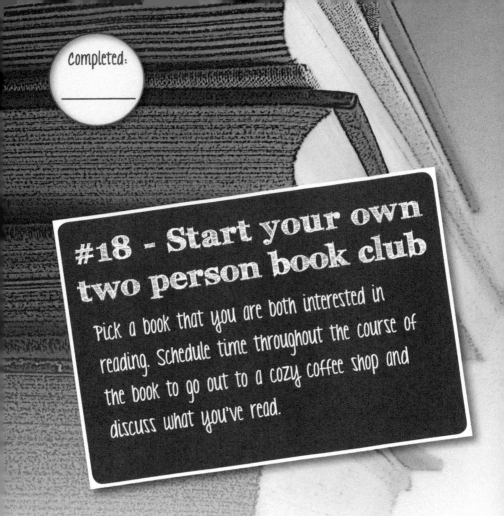

Completed:

_____

#18 - Start your own two person book club

Pick a book that you are both interested in reading. Schedule time throughout the course of the book to go out to a cozy coffee shop and discuss what you've read.

What book did you choose? Did you choose it together? _____

_____

Were your views on the book similar or different? _____

_____

What was your favorite part? _____

_____

How would you rank this? ☆☆☆☆☆ Why? _____

#19 - Step outside of the ordinary

Have a backwards day. Eat dessert for breakfast. Read a newspaper from back to front. Wear your clothes backwards. Walk backwards around the block together.

Was it difficult to do things backwards? _____

_____

Did it give you a new perspective on your daily routine? _____

_____

What was your favorite part? _____

_____

How would you rank this? ☆☆☆☆☆ Why? _____

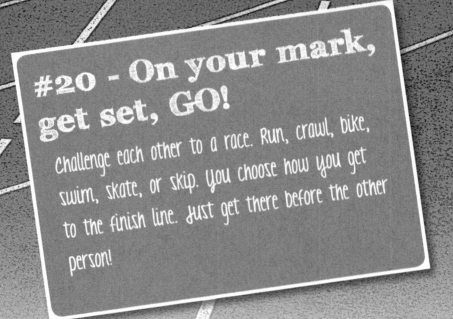

#20 - On your mark, get set, GO!

Challenge each other to a race. Run, crawl, bike, swim, skate, or skip. You choose how you get to the finish line. Just get there before the other person!

What kind of race did you choose? _____

_____

Who won?   Did you have a rematch? _____

_____

What was your favorite part? _____

_____

How would you rank this? ☆☆☆☆☆ Why? _____

#21 - Leave your decisions to chance

Make all of your decisions for the day by flipping a coin. Take turns calling heads or tails and the winner gets to call the shots for that round.

Was it hard giving up control? _____

_____

Were you happy with the other person's decisions? _____

_____

What was your favorite part? _____

_____

How would you rank this? ☆☆☆☆☆ Why? _____

Completed:

_____

#22 - Find your inner wine connoisseurs

Buy a few varieties of wine (or your alcoholic beverage of choice). Make tasting cards and record the appearance, aroma, and flavor. Compare your tasting preferences.

Are your tastes similar? _____

_____

Were you surprised by any that you thought you might not like? _____

_____

What was your favorite part? _____

_____

How would you rank this? ☆☆☆☆☆ Why? _____

Completed:
_____

#23 - Spice up your next dining experience

Go to a new restaurant and pick out something on the menu that you think your partner should try. Keep it a secret until the waiter comes, and then order for each other.

What did you order for each other? _____
_____

Were you happy with your food? _____
_____

What was your favorite part? _____
_____

How would you rank this? ☆☆☆☆☆ Why? _____

#24 - Put on your dancing shoes

Search your area for a local dance studio and take a class together. There's everything from line dancing to salsa, swing to the fox trot. Give one a whirl and see what you like.

What kind of class did you take? _____
_____

Were you naturals or did either of you have two left feet? _____
_____

What was your favorite part? _____
_____

How would you rank this? ☆☆☆☆☆ Why? _____

#25 - Eat dessert first...life is short

Show your sweet tooth some love. The next time you go out to eat, skip straight to the desserts. Order the most decadent thing on the menu, get two forks, and dig in!

Where did you go? What did you order? _____
_____

Did you share one, each order your own, or did you sample each other's?
_____

What was your favorite part? _____
_____

How would you rank this? ☆☆☆☆☆ Why? _____

#26 - Trek outside your neighborhood

Grab a couple bikes (or a bicycle built for two if you're feeling adventurous) and head to a neighboring town. Shake things up and you may just find your new favorite place to ride.

Where did you ride to? _____

_____

Did you prefer the journey or the destination? Why? _____

_____

What was your favorite part? _____

_____

How would you rank this? ☆☆☆☆☆ Why? _____

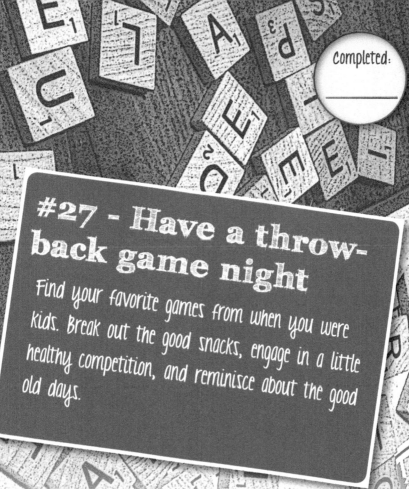

#27 - Have a throw-back game night

Find your favorite games from when you were kids. Break out the good snacks, engage in a little healthy competition, and reminisce about the good old days.

What games did you play? _____
_____

Were the games as much fun as you remembered them? _____
_____

What was your favorite part? _____
_____

How would you rank this? ☆☆☆☆☆ Why? _____

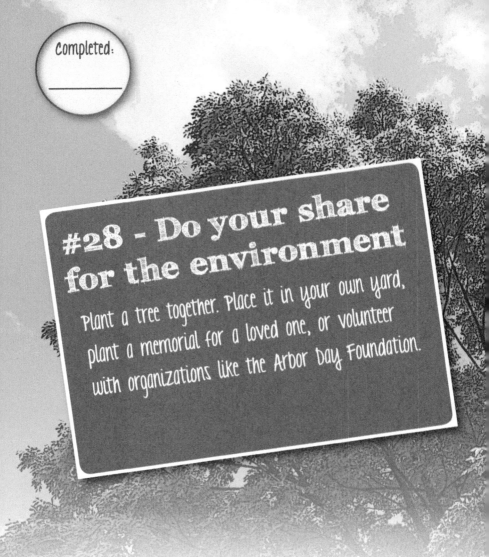

Completed:

_____

#28 - Do your share for the environment

Plant a tree together. Place it in your own yard, plant a memorial for a loved one, or volunteer with organizations like the Arbor Day Foundation.

What kind of tree did you plant? _____

_____

Where did you plant the tree? Did it have any special meaning? _____

_____

What was your favorite part? _____

_____

How would you rank this? ☆ ☆ ☆ ☆ ☆ Why? _____

#29 – Mail your love a little romance

Send your partner a formal date night invitation. Say where and when to meet and what to wear. Make reservations at a nice restaurant or have a romantic date at home.

Which of you sent out the invitation? How did the other person react?

_____

What did you end up doing? _____

_____

What was your favorite part? _____

_____

How would you rank this? ☆☆☆☆☆ Why? _____

Completed: _____

#30 - Give back to your community

Choose a cause that means something to both of you and volunteer your time. There are some great ideas at www.serve.gov and www.volunteermatch.org.

What cause did you choose to volunteer for? Why? _____
_____

How did it make you feel to volunteer your time? _____
_____

What was your favorite part? _____
_____

How would you rank this? ☆☆☆☆☆ Why? _____

#31 - Find your new favorite food/drink

The next time you place an order at a cafe or restaurant, take a risk and ask them to 'surprise us'. You might just discover something that you love and order regularly.

What food or drink were you surprised with? Did you like it? _____
_____

Were either of you afraid of what you were going to get? _____
_____

What was your favorite part? _____
_____

How would you rank this? ☆☆☆☆☆ Why? _____

Completed:
_____

#32 - Walk the runway for a cause

Go through your closets and pull out anything that you haven't worn in over a year. Put on some music and have fun modeling them for each other. Then donate the clothes to charity.

What were the craziest outfits that you had in your closets? _____
_____

Did your partner have to convince you to get rid of anything? _____
_____

What was your favorite part? _____
_____

How would you rank this? ☆☆☆☆☆ Why? _____

Completed: _____

#33 - Loan or borrow a cup of sugar

Introduce yourselves to neighbors that you've never spoken to. It never hurts to have a friendly face next door and you may just find a great new couple to hang out with!

How did the introductions go? _____

_____

Are you glad you did it? Why? _____

_____

What was your favorite part? _____

_____

How would you rank this? ☆☆☆☆☆ Why? _____

#34 - Go for the gold in your own backyard

Challenge each other to your very own version of the Olympics. Set up obstacles, yard games, and mini races. Don't forget the medals for the winner!

What events did you choose? _____

_____

Who was more competitive? _____

_____

What was your favorite part? _____

_____

How would you rank this? ☆☆☆☆☆ Why? _____

#35 - Feel the wind in your hair

Rent your dream sports car (something extravagant) and hit the highway. Drive somewhere scenic, take in some incredible views, and catch up on what's on your minds.

What kind of car did you rent? Where did you go? _____

_____

What did you see, do and talk about along the way? _____

_____

What was your favorite part? _____

_____

How would you rank this? ☆☆☆☆☆ Why? _____

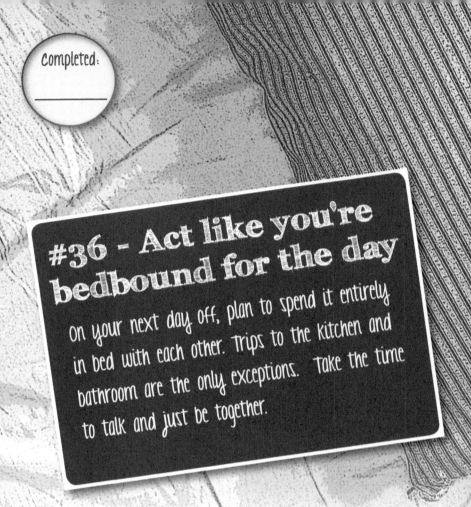

Completed:
_____

#36 - Act like you're bedbound for the day

On your next day off, plan to spend it entirely in bed with each other. Trips to the kitchen and bathroom are the only exceptions. Take the time to talk and just be together.

Was it a challenge to shut out the rest of the world? _____
_____

What did you learn about each other? _____
_____

What was your favorite part? _____
_____

How would you rank this? ☆☆☆☆☆ Why? _____

Completed:
_____

#37 - Make lemonade
...literally

Open competing lemonade stands on opposite corners in your neighborhood. Make your best lemonade and baked goods, put up signs, and see who is the most profitable.

Who made the most money? Did you strategize beforehand? _____
_____

What did you do with your earnings? _____
_____

What was your favorite part? _____
_____

How would you rank this? ☆☆☆☆☆ Why? _____

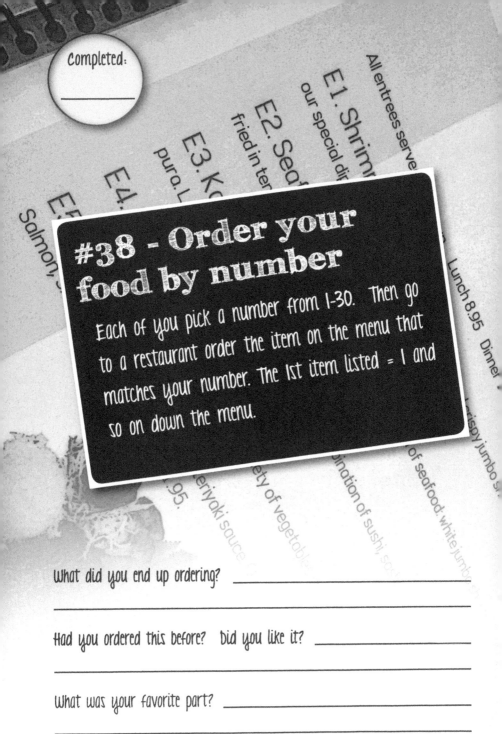

Completed:
_____

All entrees serve...

E1. Shrim...
our special dir...

E2. Sea...
fried in ter...

E3. K...
pura. L...

E4...

Salmon, ...

Lunch 8.95 Dinner ...

#38 – Order your food by number

Each of you pick a number from 1-30. Then go to a restaurant order the item on the menu that matches your number. The 1st item listed = 1 and so on down the menu.

What did you end up ordering? _____
_____

Had you ordered this before? Did you like it? _____
_____

What was your favorite part? _____
_____

How would you rank this? ☆☆☆☆☆ Why? _____

#39 - Pack your partner's bags

Find a little bed and breakfast an hour or so from home. Throw some clothes for the two of you in a bag and surprise your partner with a night away. Unwind and recharge.

Where did you go? Why did you choose this location? _____

_____

How did the other person react to the surprise? _____

_____

What was your favorite part? _____

_____

How would you rank this? ☆☆☆☆☆ Why? _____

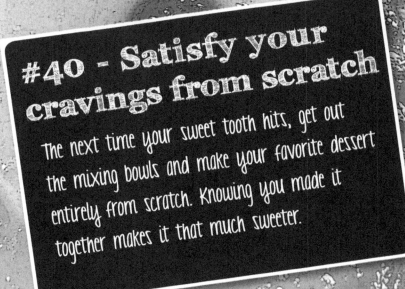

#40 - Satisfy your cravings from scratch

The next time your sweet tooth hits, get out the mixing bowls and make your favorite dessert entirely from scratch. Knowing you made it together makes it that much sweeter.

What did you make? Did you follow a recipe? _____

_____

Did it taste better than the store-bought version? _____

_____

What was your favorite part? _____

_____

How would you rank this? ☆☆☆☆☆ Why? _____

#41 - Make each other goodie bags

Fill a gift bag with some of your partner's favorite things: candy, small gifts, books, baked goods, etc. Include a note explaining why you love him or her. Exchange bags and enjoy!

What did you include in the bags? Why? _____

_____

How well did you do coming up with his/her favorite things? _____

_____

What was your favorite part? _____

_____

How would you rank this? ☆☆☆☆☆ Why? _____

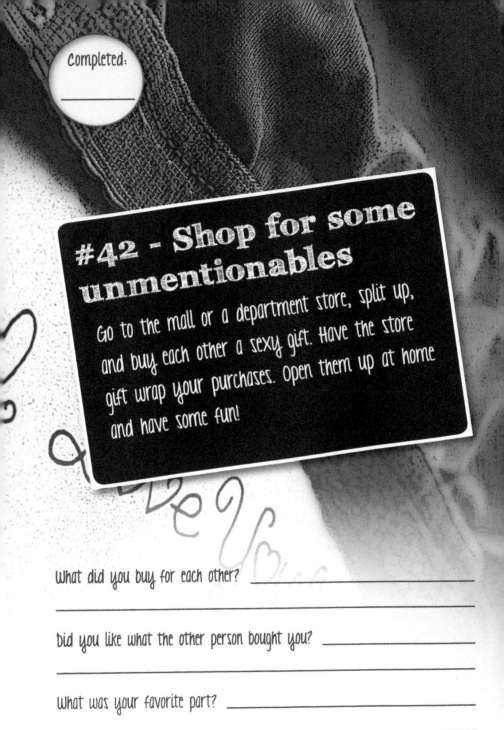

#42 - Shop for some unmentionables

Go to the mall or a department store, split up, and buy each other a sexy gift. Have the store gift wrap your purchases. Open them up at home and have some fun!

What did you buy for each other? _____

_____

Did you like what the other person bought you? _____

_____

What was your favorite part? _____

_____

How would you rank this? ☆☆☆☆☆ Why? _____

#43 - Have a luau inspired date night

Create your very own island retreat. Get out the leis, turn on some island music, make umbrella drinks, and grill kabobs. Enjoy a taste of the tropics anytime of the year.

Did you come up with any creative decorations or activities? _____

_____

Did it feel like a mini get-away? _____

_____

What was your favorite part? _____

_____

How would you rank this? ☆☆☆☆☆ Why? _____

#44 - Go halfsies on your next date idea

Show a little date night team work! One of you is responsible for the meal portion, and the other has to come up with the entertainment. Try to be creative!

What did you come up with? Was it a success? _____
_____

Who was more creative? _____
_____

What was your favorite part? _____
_____

How would you rank this? ☆☆☆☆☆ Why? _____

Completed:
_____

#45 - Break out your formal wear

Create your own prom night. Ask out your date, dress-up, buy a corsage and boutonniere, and hit the town. Go out to a nice dinner and then go dancing.

How did this compare to your high school prom? _____
_____

Where did you go to dinner? Dancing? _____
_____

What was your favorite part? _____
_____

How would you rank this? ☆☆☆☆☆ Why? _____

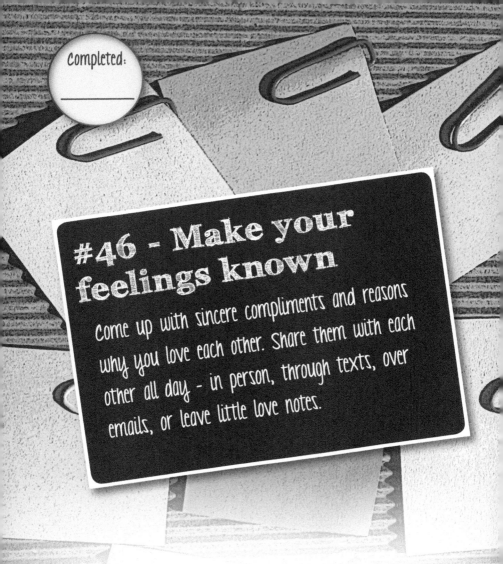

#46 - Make your feelings known

Come up with sincere compliments and reasons why you love each other. Share them with each other all day - in person, through texts, over emails, or leave little love notes.

How did your compliments and reasons compare to each other's? _____

_____

What was your favorite method of communicating and receiving them? _____

_____

What was your favorite part? _____

_____

How would you rank this? ☆☆☆☆☆ Why? _____

#47 – Leave your mark on the sidewalk

Pick up some sidewalk chalk and let your imaginations run wild. Play games like hopscotch or tick-tack-toe. Draw mazes, pictures, and signs for visitors. Take pictures of your art.

What masterpieces did you create? Did you photograph them? _____
_____

Did you let loose and have fun with it? _____
_____

What was your favorite part? _____
_____

How would you rank this? ☆☆☆☆☆ Why? _____

#48 - See things with your other senses

Let your partner blindfold you and lead you around some of your usual hang-outs. Take notice of how your experiences change. Then switch and give your partner a chance.

In what ways did familiar places change once you were blindfolded? _____

_____

Was it hard to trust your partner to see for you? _____

_____

What was your favorite part? _____

_____

How would you rank this? ☆☆☆☆☆ Why? _____

Completed:
_____

#49 - Preserve this time in your lives

Make a time capsule using a waterproof box. Place the things inside that represent your relationship at this moment. Then bury it and dig it up five years from now.

What things did you include in the time capsule? _____
_____

How do you think things will change in five years? _____
_____

What was your favorite part? _____
_____

How would you rank this? ☆☆☆☆☆ Why? _____

#50 - Imagine shapes in the clouds

On the next nice day, lay outside on your backs in the grass. Looking up at the sky, take turns calling out the people and things you see in the clouds as they pass overhead.

What shapes did you see? _____

_____

Could your partner see the same thing that you did? _____

_____

What was your favorite part? _____

_____

How would you rank this? ☆☆☆☆☆ Why? _____

Completed:
_____

#51 - Personalize your walkway

Buy a kit to make a custom stepping stone for your home or garden. Decorate it together using things you both love. Add your handprints, the date, and a personal message.

How did you choose to decorate your stone? _____

_____

Where did you decide to place it? _____

_____

What was your favorite part? _____

_____

How would you rank this? ☆☆☆☆☆ Why? _____

#52 - Change scenery between courses

Have a progressive dinner date. Choose four restaurants within walking distance of each other. Get drinks at one, appetizers at another, dinner at a third, and dessert at a fourth.

What four restaurants did you choose? _____

_____

Did you like the places you chose for each part of the meal? _____

_____

What was your favorite part? _____

_____

How would you rank this? ☆ ☆ ☆ ☆ ☆ Why? _____

#53 - Put yourself in the spotlight

Stage your own talent show at home. Sing, dance, do some magic tricks, play an instrument, etc. Impress each other with some of your little known talents.

What talents did you show off? _____

_____

What did you think of each other's talents? _____

_____

What was your favorite part? _____

_____

How would you rank this? ☆☆☆☆☆ Why? _____

Completed:
_____

#54 - Make a must-see movie list

List out a variety of movies that you and your significant other want to watch or re-watch. Set aside some time once or twice a week to cross them off your list.

What are the top five, must-see movies on your list? _____
_____

How did the repeat's compare to the first time you watched them? _____
_____

What was your favorite part? _____
_____

How would you rank this? ☆☆☆☆☆ Why? _____

#55 - Support your local musical talent

Head to a small venue, coffee shop or bar, and listen to a local band play. Try to find a group or musician that you haven't heard before and broaden your musical horizons.

Where did you go? What style of music did you hear? _____
_____

Who was the band or musician? Had you heard them before? _____
_____

What was your favorite part? _____
_____

How would you rank this? ☆ ☆ ☆ ☆ ☆ Why? _____

#56 - Team up for the Sunday challenge

Work together to finish the Sunday crossword puzzle. Start with the one in your local paper or if you're feeling ambitious go straight for the national papers.

What was the hardest clue in the puzzle? _____
_____

Were you able to finish it without cheating and using the internet? _____
_____

What was your favorite part? _____
_____

How would you rank this? ☆☆☆☆☆ Why? _____

56

#57 - Check out the view from the top

Climb to the top of the tallest building, structure, or landmark in your area and take in a bird's eye view. Notice how your perspective changes from that vantage point.

Where did you go? How high were you? _____
_____

What did you see? Could you see your home? _____
_____

What was your favorite part? _____
_____

How would you rank this? ☆☆☆☆☆ Why? _____

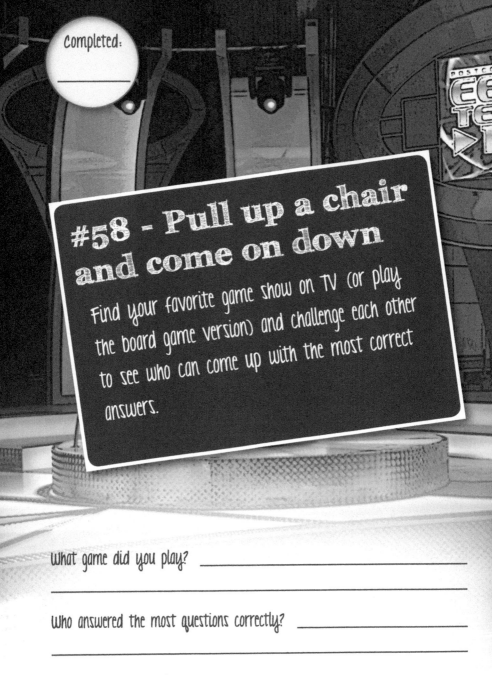

#58 - Pull up a chair and come on down

Find your favorite game show on TV (or play the board game version) and challenge each other to see who can come up with the most correct answers.

What game did you play? _____

_____

Who answered the most questions correctly? _____

_____

What was your favorite part? _____

_____

How would you rank this? ☆☆☆☆☆ Why? _____

Completed:
_____

#59 - Judge a book by its cover

Go some place crowded, like an airport, festival, or shopping center and find a spot to sit and people watch. Take turns making up stories about the lives of the people you see.

Describe some of the more interesting people you saw: _____
_____

What kinds of stories did you come up with? _____
_____

What was your favorite part? _____
_____

How would you rank this? ☆☆☆☆☆ Why? _____

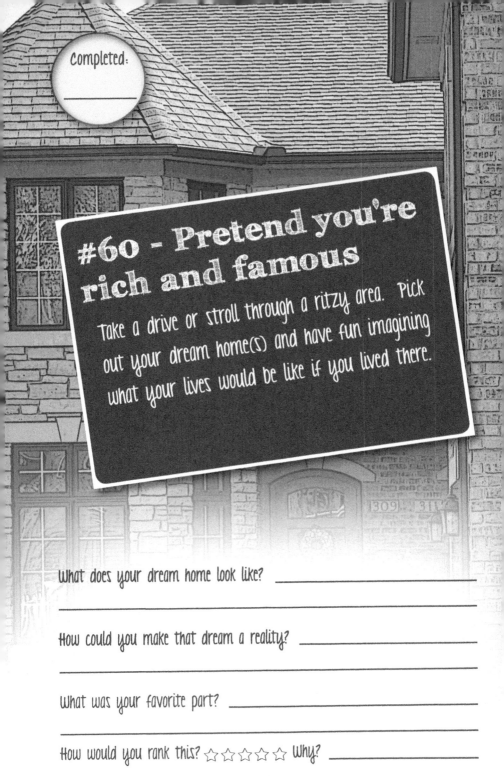

Completed:

_____

#60 - Pretend you're rich and famous

Take a drive or stroll through a ritzy area. Pick out your dream home(s) and have fun imagining what your lives would be like if you lived there.

What does your dream home look like? _____

_____

How could you make that dream a reality? _____

_____

What was your favorite part? _____

_____

How would you rank this? ☆☆☆☆☆ Why? _____

#61 - Relax and get pampered

Book a couples massage and enjoy a little bonding time while all of your cares melt away. Look for added amenities like fireplaces, comfy robes, or beach side locations.

Where did you go for your massage? _____

_____

Was it either of your first massage?   First massage together? _____

_____

What was your favorite part? _____

_____

How would you rank this? ☆☆☆☆☆ Why? _____

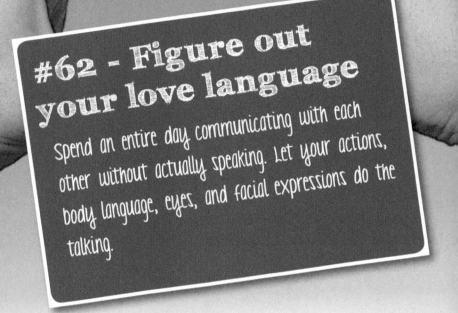

Completed:

_____

#62 - Figure out your love language

Spend an entire day communicating with each other without actually speaking. Let your actions, body language, eyes, and facial expressions do the talking.

What was the most challenging part? _____

_____

Without talking, what was the most effective way of communicating? _____

_____

What was your favorite part? _____

_____

How would you rank this? ☆☆☆☆☆ Why? _____

#63 - Coauthor a short story

Take turns writing one sentence at a time until you have a completed story. Need some inspiration to get started?   Search the internet for 'story starters'.

What did you write about? _____
_____

Why did you choose this topic? _____
_____

What was your favorite part? _____
_____

How would you rank this? ☆☆☆☆☆ Why? _____

#64 - Count to ten and go seek

Find a good hiding spot in your home and play hide and seek. You may feel silly at first, but go with it. Sometimes silly is just what you need when you're taking life too seriously.

Where was the best hiding spot you found? _____

_____

Did you let yourselves have fun? _____

_____

What was your favorite part? _____

_____

How would you rank this? ☆ ☆ ☆ ☆ ☆ Why? _____

Completed:
_____

#65 - Send those feathers flying

Have a pillow fight! Pick a day when you're both feeling a little rambunctious (preferably not angry) and let loose. First person to call uncle gets to clean up.

Who had to clean up? _____
_____

Was it a good way to let off some steam? _____
_____

What was your favorite part? _____
_____

How would you rank this? ☆☆☆☆☆ Why? _____

65

#66 - Call up friends and paint the town

Go on a pub crawl. Get some friends together and plan your own or search for pub crawls already organized in your area. It's a fun way to meet new people and see the town.

What bars/pubs did you stop at? _____

_____

Did you meet any new friends? _____

_____

What was your favorite part? _____

_____

How would you rank this? ☆☆☆☆☆ Why? _____

#67 - Take a look into your futures

Visit a psychic. Have your fortune told or your palms, tarot cards, or tea leaves read. Have fun interpreting the results. Jot down what you're told and see if it comes true.

What kind of reading did you do? _____

_____

What were you told? _____

_____

What was your favorite part? _____

_____

How would you rank this? ☆☆☆☆☆ Why? _____

#68 - Fly a kite and send it soaring

On the next windy day take a kite to an open area. One of you hold the string while the other walks downwind with the kite and then releases it into the sky. Take turns.

Did you get it to fly on your first try? _____

_____

Were you able to make the kite do any tricks? _____

_____

What was your favorite part? _____

_____

How would you rank this? ☆ ☆ ☆ ☆ ☆ Why? _____

Completed:
_____

#69 - Have some tricks up your sleeve

Master a few card or magic tricks. When you have them down, try them out on each other. See if you can figure out how the other person does his/her trick.

What kind of tricks did you learn? _____
_____

Was the other person able to figure out the trick? _____

What was your favorite part? _____

How would you rank this? ☆☆☆☆☆ Why? _____

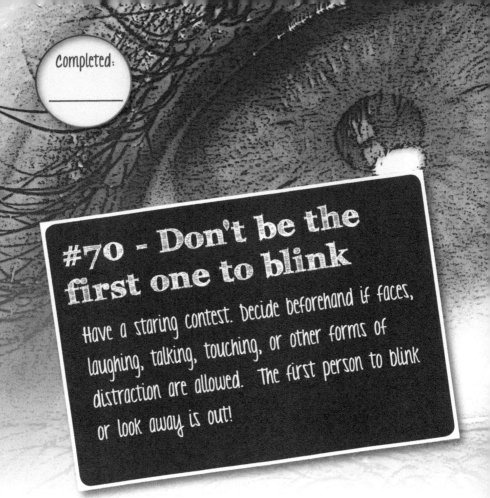

#70 - Don't be the first one to blink

Have a staring contest. Decide beforehand if faces, laughing, talking, touching, or other forms of distraction are allowed. The first person to blink or look away is out!

Who was the winner? _____

_____

What strategies did the winner use? _____

_____

What was your favorite part? _____

_____

How would you rank this? ☆ ☆ ☆ ☆ ☆ Why? _____

Completed:

_____

#71 - Try out your green thumb

Figure out the growing season for your area. Find a spot in your yard or community garden and plant some seeds. You'll be enjoying your own fresh fruits and veggies in no time.

What did you plant? _____

_____

What grew well and what would you do differently? _____

_____

What was your favorite part? _____

_____

How would you rank this? ☆☆☆☆☆ Why? _____

Completed:
_____

#72 - Float up above the clouds

Find a place that offers hot air balloon rides in your area. Many tours include champagne and an in-flight picnic. Enjoy the serene, romantic setting and incredible views.

What area did you fly over? _____

_____

What did you see? _____

_____

What was your favorite part? _____

_____

How would you rank this? ☆☆☆☆☆ Why? _____

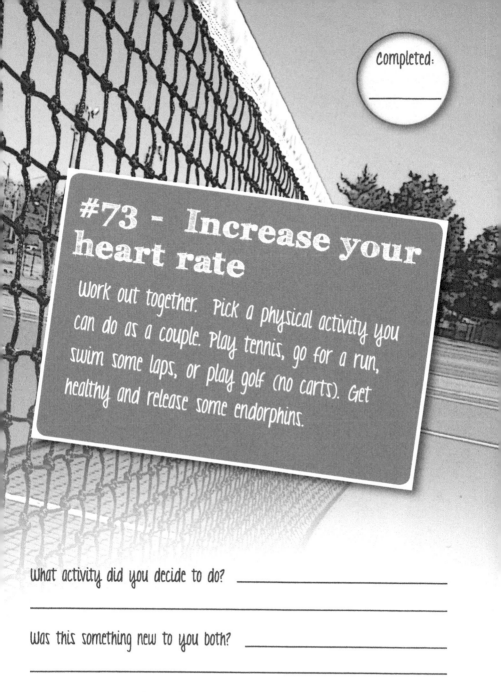

#73 - Increase your heart rate

Work out together. Pick a physical activity you can do as a couple. Play tennis, go for a run, swim some laps, or play golf (no carts). Get healthy and release some endorphins.

What activity did you decide to do? _____
_____

Was this something new to you both? _____
_____

What was your favorite part? _____
_____

How would you rank this? ☆☆☆☆☆ Why? _____

#74 – Play competitive window shopping

Walk along some store fronts. Pick out a store and try to get the other person to guess what item you spy through the window. The loser has to buy the winner a gift from the store.

What store windows did you choose? _____

_____

What gifts did you win? _____

_____

What was your favorite part? _____

_____

How would you rank this? ☆☆☆☆☆ Why? _____

#75 - Stick your toes in the sand

Grab the sunscreen, some towels, a couple of good books, and head to your nearest beach. Cuddle up by the water and just relax. Enjoy the sand and the sound of the water.

What beach did you go to? _____

_____

Was this a relaxing experience? _____

_____

What was your favorite part? _____

_____

How would you rank this? ☆☆☆☆☆ Why? _____

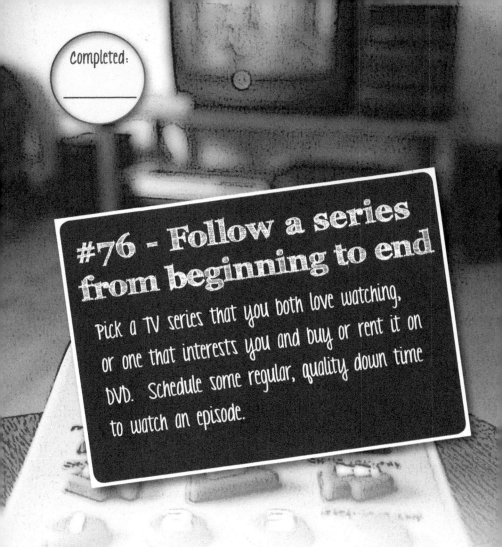

#76 - Follow a series from beginning to end

Pick a TV series that you both love watching, or one that interests you and buy or rent it on DVD. Schedule some regular, quality down time to watch an episode.

What series did you choose?   Had you watched this show before? _____

_____

Did you make it through the series? _____

_____

What was your favorite part? _____

_____

How would you rank this? ☆ ☆ ☆ ☆ ☆ Why? _____

#77 - Rise and shine before the sun

Wake up early and head to a spot in your area with an unobstructed view. Try a beach or the highest point in town. Snuggle up together and watch the sunrise.

Where did you go? _____

_____

Was it a good way to start your day? _____

_____

What was your favorite part? _____

_____

How would you rank this? ☆☆☆☆☆ Why? _____

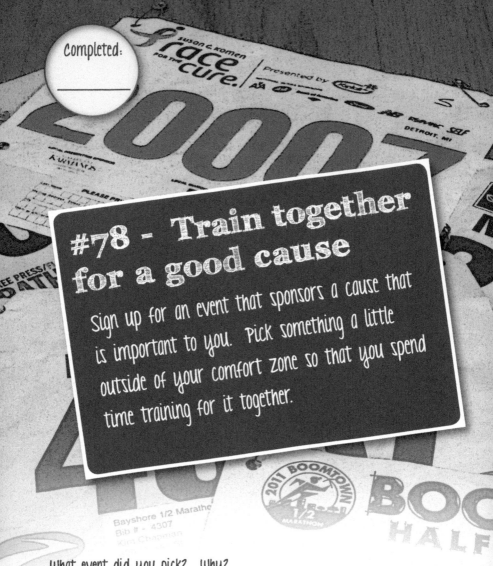

Completed: _____

#78 - Train together for a good cause

Sign up for an event that sponsors a cause that is important to you. Pick something a little outside of your comfort zone so that you spend time training for it together.

What event did you pick? Why? _____

_____

How was the training? Did you finish the event? _____

_____

What was your favorite part? _____

_____

How would you rank this? ☆☆☆☆☆ Why? _____

#79 - Lock lips for a blind taste test

Buy ten different flavors of lip balm. Divide them up without looking at who has what. Take turns putting them on and have the other person guess the flavor by kissing you.

How many did you each guess correctly? _____

_____

What was your favorite flavor? _____

_____

What was your favorite part? _____

_____

How would you rank this? ☆☆☆☆☆ Why? _____

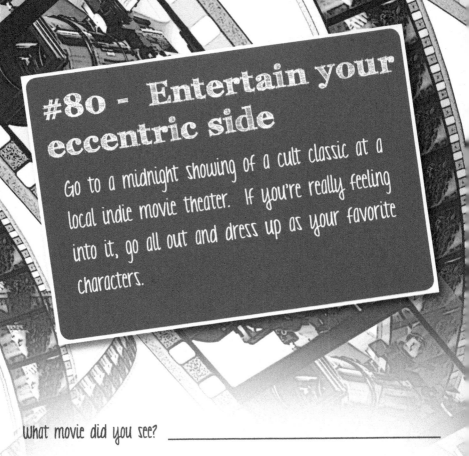

Completed:

_____

#80 - Entertain your eccentric side

Go to a midnight showing of a cult classic at a local indie movie theater. If you're really feeling into it, go all out and dress up as your favorite characters.

What movie did you see? _____

_____

Did you dress up? If so, as what? _____

_____

What was your favorite part?_____

_____

How would you rank this? ☆☆☆☆☆ Why? _____

#81 - Forget the forks and knives

Make your favorite finger foods for dinner. Lay down a blanket in your living room and have a picnic inside your house. Hand-feed each other dinner. Don't forget dessert!

What did you make? _____

_____

Did you enjoy eating on the floor without utensils? _____

_____

What was your favorite part? _____

_____

How would you rank this? ☆☆☆☆☆ Why? _____

#82 – Get ahead of the learning curve

Sign up for a continuing education class together. Look for a course you're both interested in at a local community college or through your city's community center.

What class did you choose? _____

_____

Did you learn a lot? _____

_____

What was your favorite part? _____

_____

How would you rank this? ☆☆☆☆☆ Why? _____

#83 - Become one with mother nature

Buy a wildlife guide or rent one from the library, and hit your local nature trails. Spot interesting flowers, trees, and wildlife, then look it up in the guide to learn about them.

Where did you go? _____

_____

What was the most surprising thing you learned? _____

_____

What was your favorite part? _____

_____

How would you rank this? ☆☆☆☆☆ Why? _____

Completed:

_____

#84 - Don't forget to put the cherry on top

Buy your favorite ice cream flavors and toppings and set up an ice cream sundae bar. Mix and match flavors and toppings to build each other perfect sundaes.

What sundae combinations did you try? _____

_____

What was the winning recipe? _____

_____

What was your favorite part? _____

_____

How would you rank this? ☆☆☆☆☆ Why? _____

#85 - Lean in and give your lips a workout

Practice makes perfect. Give each other 100 kisses in the span of three hours. Try for a little variety and see which kind of kisses your significant other prefers.

Describe each other's idea of a perfect kiss? _____

_____

Did you give a least 100 kisses in three hours? _____

_____

What was your favorite part? _____

_____

How would you rank this? ☆☆☆☆☆ Why? _____

Completed:

_____

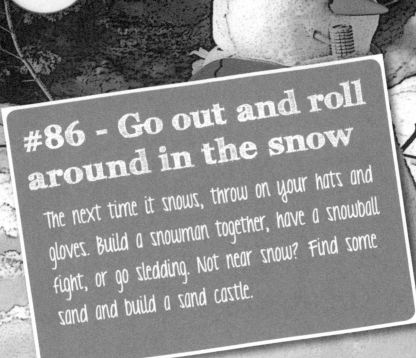

#86 - Go out and roll around in the snow

The next time it snows, throw on your hats and gloves. Build a snowman together, have a snowball fight, or go sledding. Not near snow? Find some sand and build a sand castle.

What did you do in the snow/sand? _____

_____

Did it give you a greater appreciation for cold/hot weather? _____

_____

What was your favorite part?_____

_____

How would you rank this? ☆ ☆ ☆ ☆ ☆ Why? _____

#87 - Become a little more cultured

Find an art gallery nearby and check it out. Pick out a couple of pieces that you are interested in and learn more about the style and the artist's inspiration.

What caught your attention? Why? _____

_____

What was the most interesting thing you learned? _____

_____

What was your favorite part? _____

_____

How would you rank this? ☆☆☆☆☆ Why? _____

#88 - Feel good about what you're eating

Go to a local farmers market. Pick out your favorite produce and something new. Make dinner with what you find. Feel good that it's fresh, locally grown, and healthy!

What caught your eye? _____

_____

What did you make for dinner? _____

_____

What was your favorite part? _____

_____

How would you rank this? ☆☆☆☆☆ Why? _____

#89 - Give a deserved standing ovation

Attend a production at a local community theater. It's a great way to be entertained while supporting the arts in your area. If you're feeling adventurous, try out for a show.

What show did you see? _____

_____

Were you inspired to get involved with the theater? _____

_____

What was your favorite part? _____

_____

How would you rank this? ☆☆☆☆☆ Why? _____

Completed:

_____

#90 - Don't be afraid to get a little wet

The next time it rains, go outside and play! Take a walk, jump in puddles, or grab some garbage bags and make your own slip 'n slide down a grassy hill.

How adventurous did you get? _____

_____

Was any rain gear involved? _____

_____

What was your favorite part? _____

_____

How would you rank this? ☆☆☆☆☆ Why? _____

#91 - Read first, then watch the movie

Pick a book with a film adaptation that interests you both. Read the book and then see the movie together. Compare the book to the movie and discuss which you liked best.

What book and movie did you choose? _____

_____

Which did you like best?   Why? _____

_____

What was your favorite part? _____

_____

How would you rank this? ☆☆☆☆☆ Why? _____

Completed:
_____

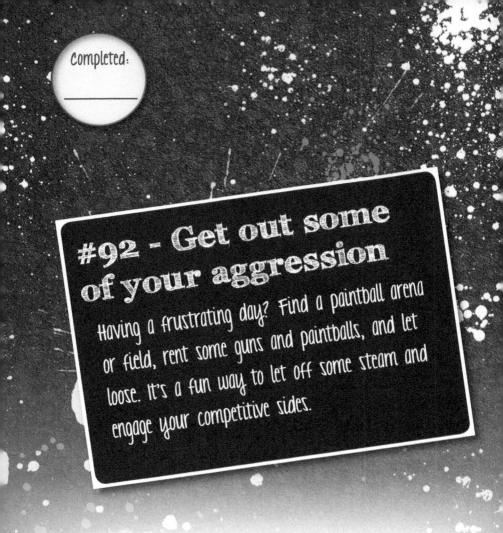

#92 - Get out some of your aggression

Having a frustrating day? Find a paintball arena or field, rent some guns and paintballs, and let loose. It's a fun way to let off some steam and engage your competitive sides.

Where did you play? _____

_____

Who escaped with the least amount of paint on them? _____

_____

What was your favorite part? _____

_____

How would you rank this? ☆☆☆☆☆ Why? _____

#93 – Cross some goals off your bucket list

Sit down and list some short-term and long-term goals you'd like to achieve. Once you have your goals written down, make a plan for how you can help each other reach them.

What are your top goals? Are they individual or goals for you as a couple?

_____

How do you plan to achieve them? _____

_____

What was your favorite part? _____

_____

How would you rank this? ☆☆☆☆☆ Why? _____

Completed:
_____

#94 - Take a ride on the hay this autumn

Take part in all those fun fall events. Go on a hay ride, pick apples, get apple cider and doughnuts, or just take a nice walk with all the colorful leaves crunching under your feet.

What fall activities did you try out? _____

_____

Did you start any new fall traditions? _____

_____

What was your favorite part? _____

_____

How would you rank this? ☆☆☆☆☆ Why? _____

94

#95 - Find the thrill-seekers within

Get your adrenaline pumping with a little adventure. Try white water rafting, bungee jumping, hang gliding, sky diving, or rock climbing. Make sure it's new to you both!

What new adventure did you try? Where did you go? _____

_____

Were you scared, excited or both? _____

_____

What was your favorite part? _____

_____

How would you rank this? ☆☆☆☆☆ Why? _____

#96 - Wear your art on your sleeve

Design your own shirts. Pick up some t-shirts, markers, paint, and transfer paper (if you want to use a photo). Decide on a design and have fun making your own wearable art.

What kind of design did you make? Do they match? _____

_____

Do you wear your shirts and show them off? _____

_____

What was your favorite part? _____

_____

How would you rank this? ☆ ☆ ☆ ☆ ☆ Why? _____

Completed:

_____

#97 - Trace back your family tree

Do a little digging online and see what you can find out about each other's family heritage. It's amazing the history you can uncover, and it's a great way to learn about each other.

How far back were you able to trace your families? _____

_____

What was the most surprising thing you learned? _____

_____

What was your favorite part? _____

_____

How would you rank this? ☆☆☆☆☆ Why? _____

97

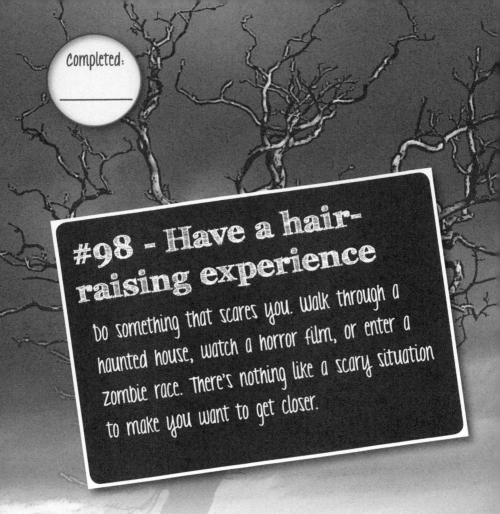

Completed:
_____

#98 - Have a hair-raising experience

Do something that scares you. Walk through a haunted house, watch a horror film, or enter a zombie race. There's nothing like a scary situation to make you want to get closer.

What scary activity did you try? _____
_____

How scared were you? Were you both freaked out? _____
_____

What was your favorite part? _____
_____

How would you rank this? ☆☆☆☆☆ Why? _____

#99 - Try a new twist on tailgating

Park folding chairs on the driveway, fire up the grill, and invite the neighbors over for your own private tailgating party. Bring your TV outside or rent a screen to catch the game.

Did you capture the stadium parking lot atmosphere? _____

_____

What was on your tailgating menu? _____

_____

What was your favorite part? _____

_____

How would you rank this? ☆☆☆☆☆ Why? _____

#100 - Discover the history all around you

Research your town and find some historical points of interest. Plan a historical walking or driving tour. Knowing the story behind your area helps you feel more connected.

What historical locations/structures did you visit? _____

_____

What was the most interesting thing you learned? _____

_____

What was your favorite part? _____

_____

How would you rank this? ☆☆☆☆☆ Why? _____

About LoveBook™

We are a group of individuals who want to spread love in all its forms. We believe love fuels the world and every relationship is important. We hope this book helps build on that belief.

www.LoveBookOnline.com

CPSIA information can be obtained
at www.ICGtesting.com
Printed in the USA
LVOW05s0104050117
519816LV00036B/529/P